Table of Contents

To Teachers and Parents

This book contains reproducible activities designed to increase skills in reading and phonics by teaching students to recognize initial and final consonant sounds. Emphasis is on listening skills to distinguish between the sounds of various letters.

Individual students may be at different levels of mastery in phonics and reading. While some may need additional review or practice, others need more challenging material to maintain interest. Phonics books are available for students at four skill levels. The activities can be used individually or in small groups.

Before students even enter first grade, they have learned much about phonics, whether they realize it or not. They may know how to spell and write their names and recognize letters of the alphabet. They have seen written material in books, magazines, and newspapers, and on signs, television, and billboards. Once they have learned the names of upper and lowercase letters and the alphabetical sequence, they are ready for more challenging material. A solid foundation in phonics enables students to increase their written and reading vocabulary.

Reading is a sequential process which encompasses many individual skills—visual discrimination, phonics clues, context clues, structural clues, sight word recognition, and listening skills. As phonics skills increase, reading ability increases, and students can enjoy more interesting books and stories.

A brief description of the skill objective for each activity is printed at the top right hand corner of each worksheet. Material is designed to be progressively more challenging. As new material is introduced, students are provided with an opportunity for practice, review, and reinforcement.

A list of student objectives is listed on the inside front cover. Extension activities provide across-the-curriculum ideas. The activities complement a variety of reading approaches and help students master basic phonics skills, enabling them to become proficient, independent readers.

Phonics books can be used with other classroom materials and a variety of teaching approaches. Activities are designed to supplement your total reading program. Appropriate phonics instruction and additional activities are important to ensure that each student has grasped all the concepts.

Extension Activities

Before handing out activities that introduce a new letter sound, discuss the sound with students. Have them suggest words that match that sound and write them on the board.

Read the directions for each page out loud to be certain students understand what is expected. To help students identify all objects, you could name the objects together before students begin working on their own.

Have students work together in groups of two or three to complete activities.

Students could cut out pictures of words that begin or end with the letter sound being studied and work together to make a collage for that sound.

Encourage students to sound out new words during oral reading class.

Take students on a "letter sound hunt." As students page through books, magazines, and catalogs, they can search for objects that begin with a specific letter. Continue the "letter hunt" on a walk through the school and playground.

Write each letter of the alphabet on a separate piece of paper. Have students take turns drawing one letter out of a hat each day. Students can suggest words that begin and end with the "letter of the day."

Students can play an alphabet matching game. Write each letter of the alphabet on individual 3 x 5 index cards. Draw objects beginning with each letter on other cards. Select several pairs of cards. Mix them up and turn them upside down. Students take turns turning over the cards to find matching pairs of letters and pictures that begin with those letters.

Randomly assign a different letter of the alphabet to each student. Ask them to bring a small item or picture to class that begins with that letter. The student can show his or her object or picture and say its name. The class can say what letter it begins with. Arrange the items in the classroom in alphabetical order.

Pages marked Review could be used as quizzes if you feel the students have sufficiently mastered the appropriate concepts. Tongue twisters are a fun way to reinforce the initial sounds of words: *Wally watched the walrus waltz; Ralph raised red roses.* Students can make up their own tongue twisters to go with the letter sound being studied.

Name _____

Start at ✱ and connect the dots in abc order.

3

Name _____

Circle letters in ABC order from left to right.

S P (A) M O B Q R C A
D H G N E V A C F W
I L G R H U T I S J
Y K Q O A L E M R N
T U X O Y Z P B C Q
R V W S U N O T E E
D F U G H V J K O P
L Z A C D C W I J L
X E I M O Y R S Z T

4   FS123256 Skill Drill Consonants

Name _____

Start at ✱ and finish the pictures in alphabetical order.

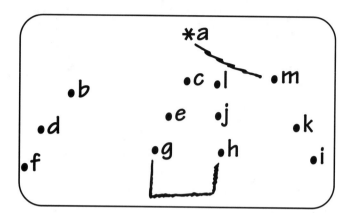

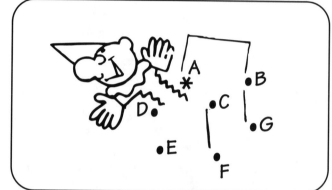

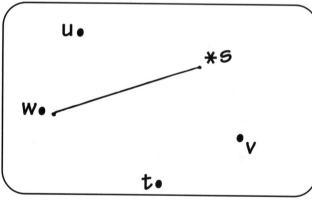

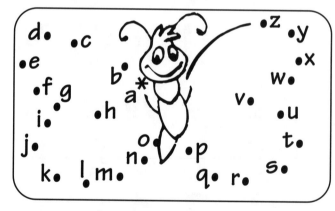

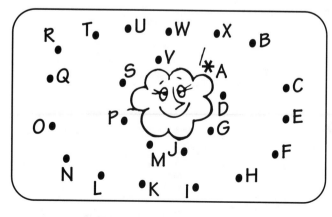

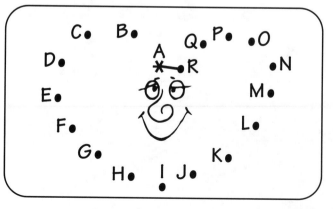

5

Name _____

In each box, write the letters that go before
and after the given letter.

u

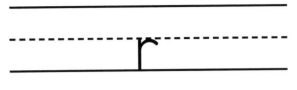

r

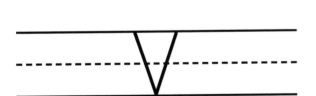

w

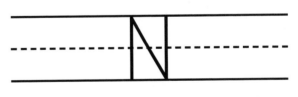

o

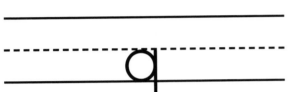

q

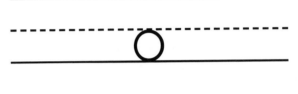

y

V

N

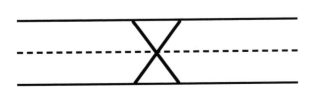

P

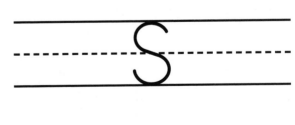

S

X

I

Name _____

Bug begins with the sound of the letter **b**. If the picture begins like ⬡, write **Bb** under the picture.

bug

B   b

Bb			

Name _____

Color the balloons with pictures that begin with the
sound of the letter **b** blue. Color the rest green.

Bb

Name _____

Turtle begins with the sound of the letter **t**. If the picture begins like 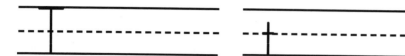, write **Tt** under the picture.

turtle

FS123256 Skill Drill Consonants

Name _____

Color the towels with pictures that begin with the sound of the letter **t** yellow. Color the rest orange.

Name _____

Seal begins with the sound of the letter **s**. If the picture begins like , write **Ss** under the picture.

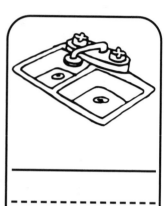

seal

- - - S - - - - - - - - - - - - - - - - - S - - - - - - - - - - - - -

- - - Ss -

- -

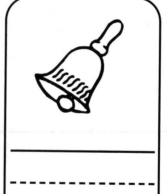

- -

FS123256 Skill Drill Consonants

Name _____

Say the name of each picture. Write the letter that
makes the sound you hear at the beginning.

b   t   s

Name _____

Mushroom begins with the sound of the letter **m**. If the picture begins like , write **Mm** under the picture.

mushroom

M _ _ _ _ _ _ _   m _ _ _ _ _ _ _

Mm

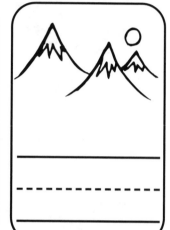

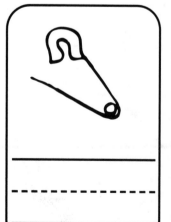

13   FS123256 Skill Drill Consonants

Name _____

Color all pictures that begin with the sound
of the letter **m** brown. Color the rest yellow.

Mm

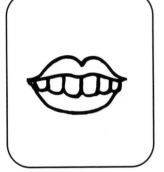   

14

Name _____

Caterpillar begins with the sound of the letter **c**. If the picture begins like , write **Cc** under the picture.

caterpillar

--C----------   --c----------

Cc

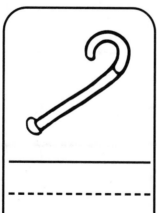

FS123256 Skill Drill Consonants

Name _____

Circle the pictures that begin with the sound of **c**. Put an X on the rest.

 Cc

Name _____

Parrot begins with the sound of the letter **p**. If the picture begins like , write **Pp** above the picture.

parrot

P _____   p _____

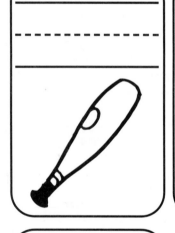

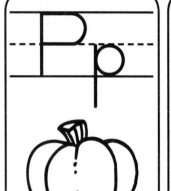

FS123256 Skill Drill Consonants

Name _____

Color the pumpkins with pictures that begin with the
sound of the letter **p** orange. Color the rest yellow.

Pp

Name _____

Say the name of each picture. Circle the letter that makes
the sound you hear at the beginning of each word.

(m)ushroom   (c)aterpillar   (p)arrot

m   c   (p)   m   c   p   m   c   p

m   c   p   m   c   p   m   c   p

m   c   p   m   c   p   m   c   p

m   c   p   m   c   p   m   c   p

m   c   p   m   c   p   m   c   p

Name _____

Say the name of each picture. Put an X on the pictures that begin
with the same sound as the letter in the first box.

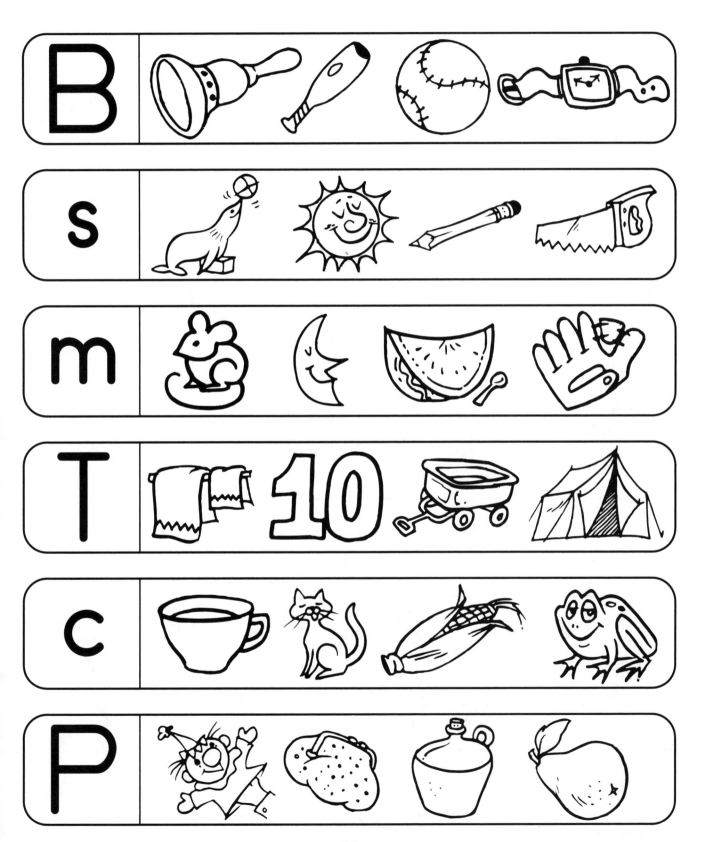

Name _____

Doll begins with the sound of the letter **d**. If the picture begins like  , write **Dd** under the picture.

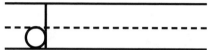

doll

FS123256 Skill Drill Consonants

Name _____

Color the toys that begin with the sound of the letter **d** purple. Color the rest red.

Dd

Name _____

Nurse begins with the sound of the letter **n**. If the picture
begins like 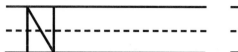, write **Nn** under the picture.

N _____ n _____

nurse

Nn

23

Name _____

Circle the pictures that begin with the
sound of **n**. Put an X on the rest.

Nn

nurse

  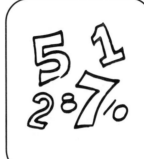 

FS123256 Skill Drill Consonants

Name _____

Lion begins with the sound of the letter l. If the picture begins like 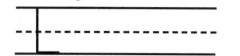, write Ll under the picture.

lion

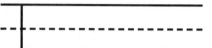

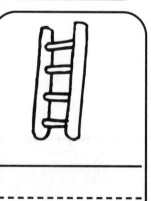

FS123256 Skill Drill Consonants

Name _____

Say the name of each picture. Write the letter that
makes the sound you hear at the beginning.

doll   nurse   lion

Name _____

Fish begins with the sound of the letter **f**. If the picture begins like 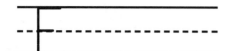 , write **Ff** under the picture.

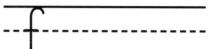
fish

F _____   f _____

Ff

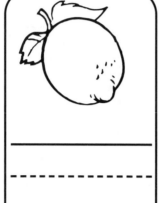

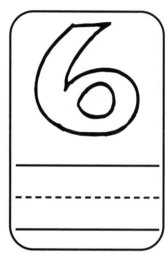

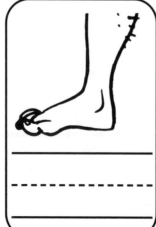

27

FS123256 Skill Drill Consonants

Name _____

Circle the pictures that begin with the
sound of **f**. Put an X on the rest.

Ff

   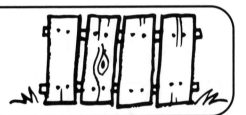

   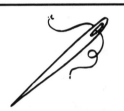

28

Name _____

Queen begins with the sound of the letter **q**. If the picture begins like , write **Qq** under the picture.

queen

_____Q_____   _____q_____

Qq

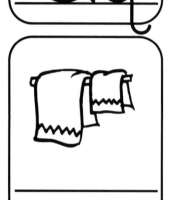

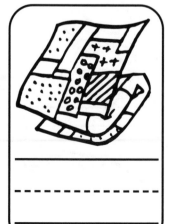

29

Name _____

Watch begins with the sound of the letter **w**. If the picture
begins like 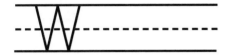, write **Ww** under the picture.

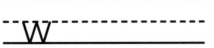

watch

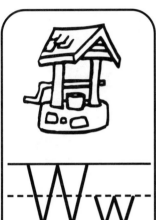

Ww

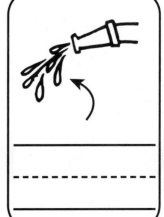

30

FS123256 Skill Drill Consonants

Name _____

Robot begins with the sound of the letter **r**. If the picture begins like , write **Rr** under the picture.

robot

R _____   r _____

Rr _____

_____

_____

_____

_____

_____

_____

_____

_____

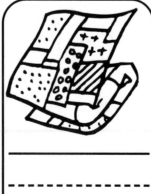

_____

_____

_____

FS123256 Skill Drill Consonants

Name _____

Find and color all the objects that begin with the sound of **r**.

Rr

FS123256 Skill Drill Consonants

Name _____

Say the name of each picture. Circle the letter that makes the sound you hear at the beginning of each word.

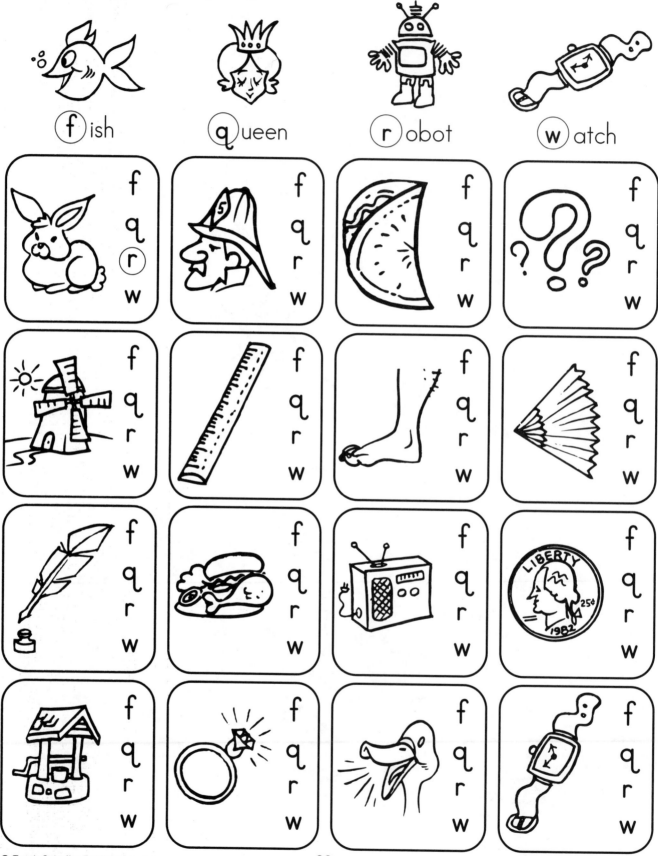

(f)ish   (q)ueen   (r)obot   (w)atch

Name _____

Look at the letter at the beginning of each row. Find
and color the pictures that begin with that letter.

R

q

w

f

I

N

D

34

FS123256 Skill Drill Consonants

Name _____

Goat begins with the sound of the letter **g**. If the picture begins like  , write **Gg** under the picture.

goat

G _____   g _____

Gg

_____

_____

_____

FS123256 Skill Drill Consonants

Name _____

Color all the golf balls with pictures that begin with the
sound of the letter **g** green. Color the rest blue.

FS123256 Skill Drill Consonants

Name _____

Hippo begins with the sound of the letter **h**. If the picture begins like 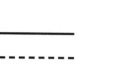 , write **Hh** under the picture.

hippo

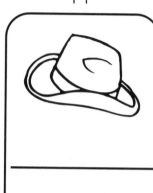

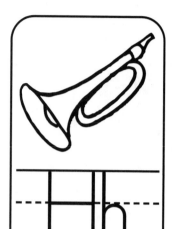

H h

37

Name _____

Circle the pictures that begin with the
sound of **h**. Put an X on the rest.

Hh

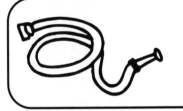   

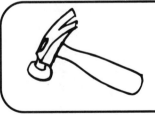   

FS123256 Skill Drill Consonants

Name _____

Kite begins with the sound of the letter **k**. If the picture begins like 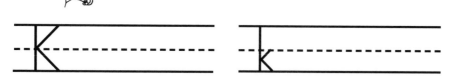 , write **Kk** under the picture.

kite

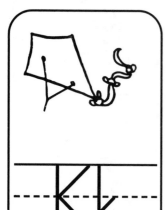

Kk

FS123256 Skill Drill Consonants

Name _____

Color the kites with pictures that begin with the sound of **k** orange. Color the others purple.

Kk

Color the pictures that begin with the sound of **g** green, **h** blue, and **k** yellow.

g h k

Name _____

Jet begins with the sound of the letter **j**. If the picture
begins like [image], write **Jj** under the picture.

J - - - - - - - - - - - - - - - - -

j - - - - - - - - - - - - - - - - -

jet

Jj

Name _____

Color the balls with pictures that begin with
the sound of **j** red. Color the rest orange.

Jj

FS123256 Skill Drill Consonants

Name _____

Violin begins with the sound of the letter **v**. If the picture begins like 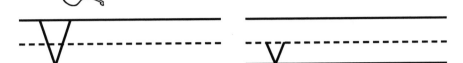, write **Vv** under the picture.

violin

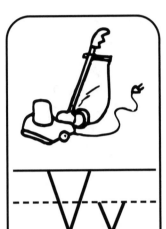 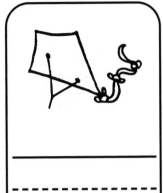  

Vv

Say the name of the picture. Write the letter that makes the sound you hear at the beginning of each word.

Name _____

Say the name of each picture.
Circle the letter that makes the
sound you hear at the beginning
of each word.

Vv Jj Yy Xx Zz

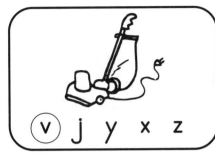

(v) j y x z

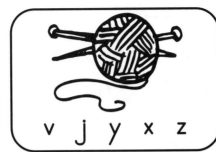

v j y x z

V j y x z

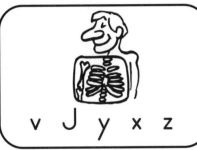

v J y x z

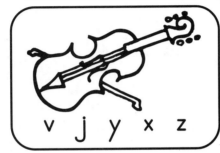

v j y x z

v j Y x z

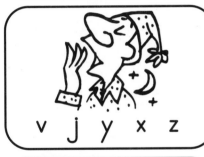

v j y x z

v j y x z

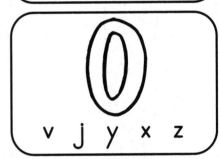

v j y x z

v j y x z

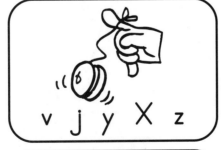

v j y X z

v j y x z

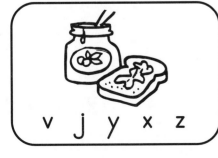

v j y x z

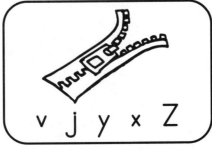

v j y x Z

v j y x z

46

Name _____

Say the name of each picture. Write the letter
that makes the sound you hear at the
beginning of each word.

Say the name of each picture. Write the sound you hear at
the end of each word.

mo(p)   bu(s)   gu(m)

Name _____

Color the tops that have pictures that end
with **p** green, **s** orange, and **m** red.

p s m

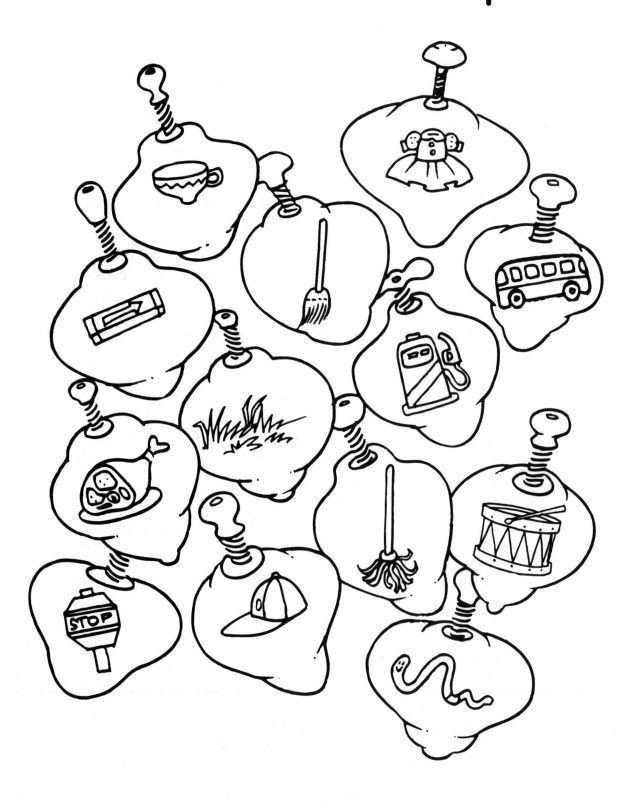

Say the name of each picture. Write the beginning and ending sounds.

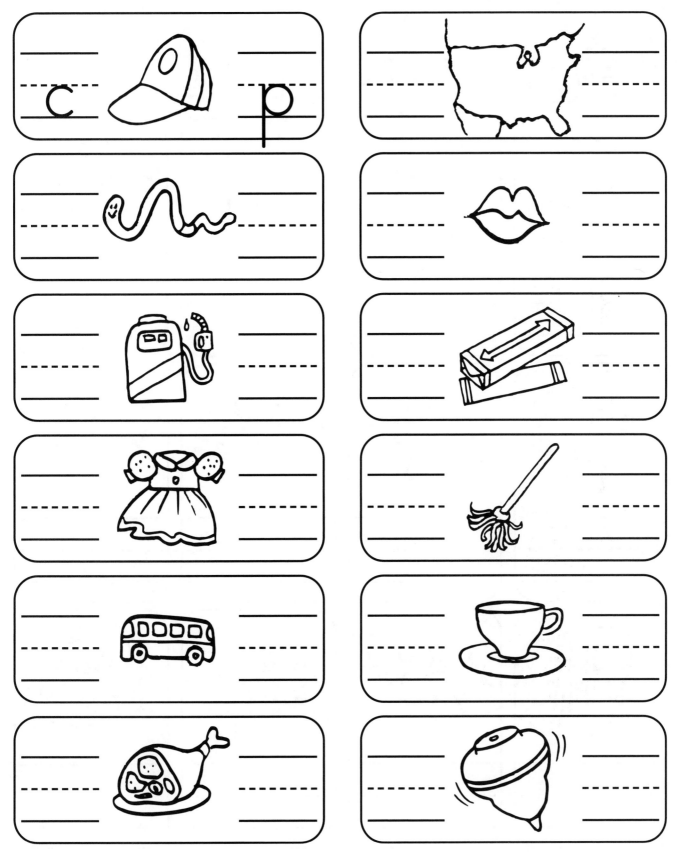

Name _____

Say the name of each picture. Write the sound you
hear at the end of each word.

 **t d r**

 cat be d ca r

_____
_ _ _ _ _ _ _ _
t
_____

_____
_ _ _ _ _ _ _ _
_____

_____
_ _ _ _ _ _ _ _
_____

_____
_ _ _ _ _ _ _ _
_____

_____
_ _ _ _ _ _ _ _
_____

_____
_ _ _ _ _ _ _ _
_____

_____
_ _ _ _ _ _ _ _
_____

_____
_ _ _ _ _ _ _ _
_____

_____
_ _ _ _ _ _ _ _
_____

_____
_ _ _ _ _ _ _ _
_____

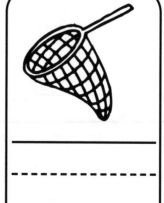

_____
_ _ _ _ _ _ _ _
_____

_____
_ _ _ _ _ _ _ _
_____

FS123256 Skill Drill Consonants

Name _____

Say the name of each picture. Circle the
sound you hear at the end of each word.

(t) d r

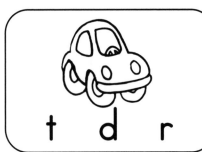
t d r

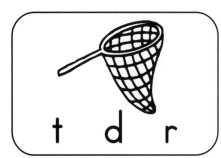
t d r

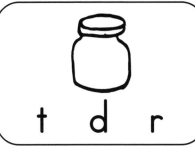
t d r

t d r

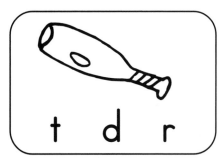
t d r

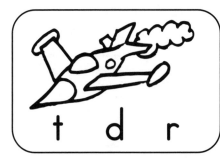
t d r

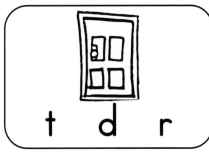
t d r

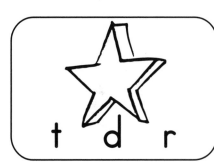
t d r

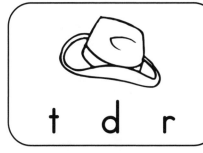
t d r

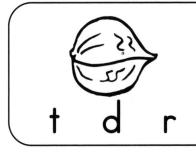
t d r

t d r

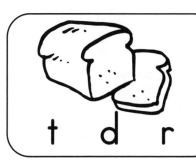
t d r

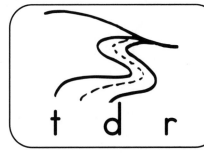
t d r

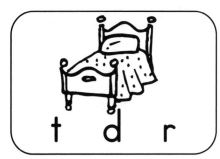
t d r

FS123256 Skill Drill Consonants

Say the name of each picture. Write the beginning and ending sounds.

Name _____

Say the name of each picture. Write the sound
you hear at the end of each word.

n b k

**10**te**n**   we**b**   boo**k**

_____

- - - - - - - - - - - -

_____

_____

- - - - - - - - - - - -

_____

_____

- - - - - - - - - - - -

_____

_____

- - - - - - - - - - - -

_____

_____

- - - - - - - - - - - -

_____

_____

- - - - - - - - - - - -

_____

_____

- - - - - - - - - - - -

_____

_____

- - - - - - - - - - - -

_____

_____

- - - - - - - - - - - -

_____

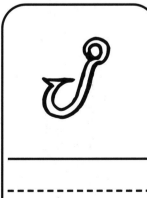

_____

- - - - - - - - - - - -

_____

_____

- - - - - - - - - - - -

_____

_____

- - - - - - - - - - - -

_____

54

Final Consonants n, b, k

Color the pictures that end with the sound
of **n** red, **b** blue, and **k** yellow.

n b k

Name _____

Say the name of each picture. Write the beginning and ending sounds.

Say the name of each picture. Write the letter that makes
the sound you hear at the end of the word.

lea f   fro g   pai l   6 si x

g

Name _____

Say the name of each picture. Circle the sound
you hear at the end of the word.

g l (f) x

g l f x

g l f x

g l f x

g l f x

g l f x

g l f x

g l f x

g l f x

g l f x

g l f x

g l f x

g l f x

g l f x

g l f x

g l f x

g l f x

g l f x

g l f x

g l f x

FS123256 Skill Drill Consonants

Say the name of each picture. Write the beginning and ending sounds.

Name _____

Say the name of each picture. Draw a line
from the beginning sound to the ending sound.

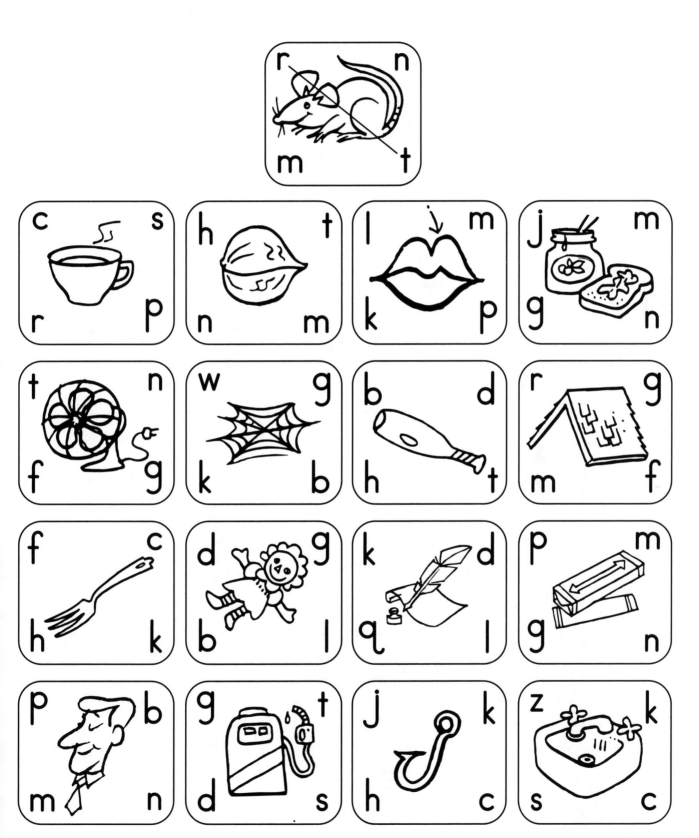

Name _____

Say the name of each picture. Draw a line from the beginning sound to the ending sound.

c ———— n
k   m
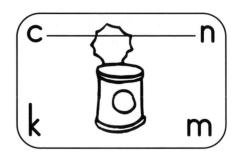

n   p
m   d
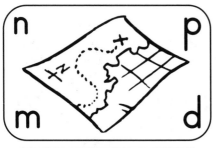

g   n
c   r

b   g
d   c

b   t
k   n

w   l
v   n

r   t
n   f

y   m
v   n

b   t
h   f

v   n
y   m

w   t
r   n

q   l
k   t

b   n
p   t

s   c
n   m

t   b
n   p

b   v
d   x
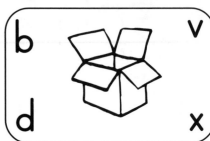

FS123256 Skill Drill Consonants

Name _____

Say the name of each picture. If it begins with the sound of
the letter in the box, color the picture purple. If it ends with
the sound of the letter in the box, color the picture green.

w
q
g
c

x
r
m
v

j
d
s
y

b
z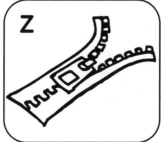
f
t

FS123256 Skill Drill Consonants

GREAT JOB!

_____

has learned the
Consonants!

Signed _____ Date _____

FS123256 Skill Drill Consonants